TABLE OF CONTENTS

Note from the author

Although this short story is a work of fiction, it is based on a true story from my own life. I believe that quite often dogs that we have loved and that have loved us return to us in different forms. With this belief, I carry the memory of each and every one of the dogs that I have loved in my heart forever. At the time of this writing Riley is curled up beside me where I hope he will be for some time to come.

On Feb. 10, a dog named Cujo was surrendered to the Westfield animal shelter. Also on Feb 10. in a Westfield home, a dog named Codi said his final goodbye to the family he had loved for over 10 years. This is the story of their connected souls.

Chapter 1: Codi

It had been a long day of whining, grumpy kids. Providing home daycare
was a job that Karen usually loved, but today had been one of those days that
made her wonder if she wasn't getting too old for it all. She was over 50,
after all! And she had been doing this job for nearly thirty years! She also
knew that a lot of how she was feeling had to do with it being winter and the
fact that everybody was suffering from a bit of cabin fever. Just the same,
whatever the reason, it was starting to wear her down. But as it did every
day, the hands of the clock finally made their way to 6 and the last tired child
was sent off in the loving arms of equally weary parents. "Just a bit of clean
up to do," Karen thought to herself, and she could begin her evening.

The first thing on the agenda every night was a walk with Codi, her Spaniel,
Border collie cross. He was a shaggy little thing, all brown, black and white
fur, with a long tail, floppy ears and short stocky legs. The kids had picked
him from the litter for just that reason. They laughed at how his little legs
couldn't even get him up the first steps of the front porch. They also loved his
chubby little puppy belly which he had somehow never managed to outgrow.

But short legs or not, he was always ready for a walk, and he did his best to
make sure it was never forgotten. For that reason alone, Karen's daily
routine seldom changed. Every night after she shut off the lights, closed the
door and headed upstairs from the daycare, he would be in the exact same
spot. She knew he would be there, waiting at the top of the stairs, stretched
out with front paws dangling down over the top step, nosed pressed against
the gate, tail sweeping a clean spot across the hardwood floor, and eyes bright
with anticipation.

"Are we going now?" he seemed to say. "I've been waiting for you. Let's
go."

And regardless of how tired she was, or what kind of a day it had been, she
couldn't resist those eyes. She would bundle up for the cold and snow while
Codi watched and waited. He never seemed to quite understand what took
her so long or why she had to put on so many things in order to go out when
he was always at the ready to just run out the door.

"If I had your fur coat," she would say, "I could just walk out the door too!"

But he would wait patiently knowing that eventually she would be ready. It was with these thoughts in mind that Karen finally flicked off the last light switch and closed the downstairs door. As she came around the landing to head upstairs, she was surprised to see that Codi wasn't there. "Where are you old fellow?" she called. "This winter weather got you down too? Am I going to get a reprieve from walking today?"

When even her cheerful comments didn't bring him to the top of the stairs, Karen began to worry. At 10, Codi was getting on and he had been moving a bit slower these past few months. The deep, thawing snow posed a particularly difficult challenge for his short little legs this time of year. At times she would almost have to lift his back end out of the snow if he sank down too far. But he was a determined fellow, and he loved his walks! So it was quite natural for Karen to be concerned when he wasn't waiting there ready to go. Karen continued to the top of the stairs and unlatched the child gate at the top.

"Codi!" she called. "Ready for a walk?" Now she could see him. He was lying in the center of the carpet looking at her and wagging his tail but making no move to get up. "What's wrong Codi? Come here boy. It's walk time." Karen tapped her leg in a typical come here motion. The response she received was not at all what she had hoped for. She watched with dismay as Codi tried to stand up and come to her. Struggle as he might, he couldn't get up on all four legs. He could drag his back end but he couldn't stand. His eyes were still the same, full of hope and anticipation but there was something else there too, a sadness maybe, or perhaps an apology. Like he was trying to tell her that he wasn't going to be able to make it this time; that things weren't going to be the same anymore. Karen fell to her knees beside him, stroking his head and feeling the tears start to come.

"Oh buddy, what's happened? You were fine this morning. You were fine when I let you out this afternoon." Karen just sat there on the floor for the longest time, crying and petting her beloved companion. When Will, her husband came in from work, that is how he found them. Trying not to cry, Karen explained the situation and Will called their vet at the Westfield Animal Hospital. Dr. Jameson agreed to see them, and made the arrangements for Codi to come in for an emergency examination. Karen's heart sank as she watched Will carry that furry ball of love out to the car. She knew it was bad. She felt it down to the depths of her soul. And she knew that Codi felt it too. In just the blink of an eye, things were suddenly so different. There was no denying the fact that life was going to change tonight forever.

Will returned in less than an hour. He carried Codi in and placed him on his bed in the corner of the living room. The news was every bit as bad as Karen had known it would be. Dr. Jameson had told Will that a nerve was severed in Codi's spine and that his back legs could no longer function. It was possible, he said, that the strain of walking through the deep snow may have accelerated a condition that had already began to progress. Or it may have happened suddenly one time when he slipped trying to get up. There was no way to ever know for sure. The fact of the matter was, he couldn't stand, couldn't walk, and basically couldn't get around except by dragging his back end. The good news was that he was not in any pain. Surgery was an option, albeit a very expensive one, and would require the amputation of both back legs. Codi would then need to be fitted for a custom cart that would hold up his back end and roll forward as he moved his front legs. It seemed like a very complicated and unnatural way to move.

The vet was blunt and told Karen and Will to consider very carefully what Codi's quality of life would be like. And in addition to all of that, there was Codi's age to consider. Also, as Dr. Jameson pointed out, Codi had never quite been back to normal from the bladder stone surgery he had had the year before. His system was not as good as it might need to be to face surgery. The vet was being honest when he told them of the risks of the surgery and the chance that Codi's system would not be able to withstand the stress. The other option, of course, was putting Codi down. Neither Karen nor Will wanted to make that final call. They had been down this road before but never had they ended up there so suddenly and without any mental preparation. This time there was no lengthy illness or failing health to give them some time to adjust to what was coming. This time they had to make the call even when everything else about their beloved friend seemed perfectly fine. Everything except the fact that he could no longer walk!

But in the end, to do their best by their faithful, loyal friend, that was the decision they made.

They made the appointment for the following morning and took Codi home for one last goodbye from the rest of the family. The ride home was quiet and their hearts were heavy. This would be their last night together. Once they were in and had Codi settled on a blanket in the living room, Karen started making calls to her daycare parents. Daycare would be cancelled for the next day. Fortunately it was a Friday, so the weekend would be free as well. With business matters taken care of, they sat quietly together reminiscing about Codi's puppy days, his antics growing up, and all the wonderful ways in which he had enriched their lives. One by one the children went off to bed and Karen and Will sat with Codi a while longer. It was difficult getting him outside to relieve himself, but they did their best. Cody knew things weren't right. He sensed the sadness that now filled the house that was usually so happy and he knew that he was the reason. He tried with his eyes to let them know that everything would be ok. That they were making the right decision and one that he was grateful for. He so wished he could talk to them and tell them that he was looking forward to crossing over the Rainbow Bridge. He was full of anticipation of things to come. But he wanted to tell them too, that he was sorry to be leaving them. He also wanted to somehow let them know, that even though he would no longer be with them as the dog they knew, he would be with them still through the spirit of a dog that they were soon to know.

But sadly, dogs have no voice for human language. So he lay quietly, accepting their hugs and scratches, returning their love as best he could with a gentle lick of the hand or a paw resting on their leg. It was a long, strange night for Codi and his family, one of the longest Karen could remember. But when morning came, they went together to say their final goodbyes.

Chapter 2: Cujo

It was just before 9 when Becky drove into the parking lot of the Westfield animal shelter. A light winter rain was falling and coated her windshield between swooshes of the wipers. As she got closer, her stomach tightened at the sight of the large crate sitting beside the door. "Looks like we have another one," she said to herself. Though she had worked at the shelter for over eight years, she never got used to the way people could just abandon an animal that they had owned and cared for.

She didn't understand why people couldn't at least bring the dogs into the shelter instead of just dropping them off when the shelter was closed. There was never enough information about the surrendered animal when they did it this way. There would be so little information to pass along to perspective new owners. Nothing about his personality that would help match him up with the right family. Nothing, either good or bad that they could use to help make him more adoptable, to increase his chances of finding that perfect, happy forever home that he so deserved. Nothing. Just a few words scratched on a piece of paper. Sometimes they didn't even get that. It was always so sad when it happened this way.

She hoped he had only been there a while and not all night. She opened the car door and walked slowly towards the large wire cage "Hello there big guy," Becky said in a calm voice, as she approached the cage. "Aren't you a handsome fellow?" He was a fairly large dog and obviously of mixed breed. He sported black, brown and white markings very similar to a Bernese mountain dog, but with a more slender build. His nose looked almost like that of a German shepherd, but his ears were all floppy like a retriever. He was tall with a long black tail and fuzzy tan britches. The most unusual thing about him was the one ear that sat sideways atop his head as though it had forgotten which way to go. It gave the dog a very bewildered look that made you want to hug him all the more. "Well now," said Becky, "Let's just see what this note says about you."

Scrawled on a small piece of paper tied to the wire crate were these few words: "This dogs' name is Cujo. He is almost a year old and just got too big for our house and our kids. I hope you can find him a good home. Thanks."

That's it. That's all she wrote. Becky sighed and looked into the sad brown eyes and wondered what his story really was, and why on earth anyone would name a family pet Cujo! He certainly looked anything but mean or aggressive.

"Oh well," she thought. "Doesn't really matter. From here on in it's you and me and the rest of the staff. And hopefully, soon a new home with new owners."

There was a long red leash attached to the black collar around the dog's neck. Becky talked to him for a bit just to judge his reaction to her presence. When it appeared he was going to be quite docile, she slowly opened the door of the crate, talking in a reassuring tone the whole time. Cujo made no move to exit the crate, even when Becky tugged gently on the leash and urged him to come. It was obvious he had trust issues and was afraid of new situations. Becky knew that patience would be the key. She just kept talking and gradually came close enough to pat his head. When he immediately drew back, Becky did too.

"Ok fella," she said, "nobody here is going to hurt you. Let's just get you out of this crate and inside the shelter." She wanted to get him in and settled before all the staff started to arrive. She had a sense that the chatter and bustle of everyone coming in might really scare this poor guy. With a bit more coaxing she was able to get him to walk with her. They stopped briefly by the walk and Cujo relieved himself on the bushes. "There you go," said Becky. "See, everything is ok. You are going to be fine. We're going to take really good care of you."

Cujo was glad to get out of the crate and stretch. He had been scared and cold sitting there all by himself, wondering if anyone was going to come. Even when his people had shut him in the small room every day, it had not been as lonely as being outside in the cold dark of early morning. He wondered where his people had gone, and why they had left him here. Would they return to take him home soon? Didn't they want him anymore? He had tried to be a good dog. He had stayed quiet in the small space every day, never barking or scratching at the door. He even tried not to urinate if he could help it, but sometimes the days were just too long and he had to go. When that happened, he always went to the farthest corner of the small place, and only as often as was absolutely necessary. He never wanted to make his people unhappy.

Lately, though, he had heard the woman person complaining that he was getting too big. He had always felt in his heart that she was unhappy with him, and kind of angry with the man for bringing him home."He is way too big to play with the kids now," she would say. "And way too big for this tiny house." This made him very sad. He loved to play with his kids and always tried to be extra careful. But maybe he hadn't been careful enough. Maybe the woman person had finally had enough and now they had left him here.

He didn't know where or what this place was, but this kind girl who was taking him out of the crate seemed very nice and gentle. Her soft voice was comforting and he wasn't afraid of her at all. The room where she took him was warm, and bright. It was clean and yet still smelled of lots of other dogs and animals. He was somewhat confused by the feelings that were coming at him from the other dogs. There seemed to be both a sense of hope and of sadness.

Later during his time here, he would learn the reason for those two emotions. There was a sense of gladness for those friends that had moved on to new homes and families, and a sorrowful kind of hope for those who were granted passage to a different place. Although their lives here on this earth had been cut short, they would now able to move forward to a new place; a place where they could begin their journey across the rainbow bridge to the land where all dogs live free from worry, illness and pain. Cujo knew that it was his time now to sit and wait. In the end, it would be one or the other of those same fates that would be his. For now, though, he was happy to be safe, warm and cared for in what he chose to call his "in between" place. The place he heard others refer to as "the shelter."

Chapter 3: Grieving

It was a warm day for mid February and raining lightly when Karen and Will pulled into the animal hospital parking lot. The smell of spring was in the air, a smell that usually brought a sense of new beginnings and anticipation of summer. But not today. Today it seemed unfair that the weather should be so nice. A bitter cold blustery day would better suit their mood for sure. When they arrived at the hospital, Karen stood in the rain and talked to Codi through the opened back hatch of their SUV. He was curled up on his favorite blanket sniffing in great gulps of the spring like air.

His eyes never left Karen's as they tried so hard to communicate their last thoughts to each other. Codi wanted her to know that he was ok. That this was how things were meant to be, and that soon, they would find themselves comforted by the love of a new canine companion.

Karen wanted Codi to know how much she loved him, would always love him; and that he had done a wonderful job as a friend, guardian and companion. She stroked his head gently and waited for Will to return. He had gone ahead to find out where the vet wanted them to take Codi with as little exposure as possible to the other waiting patients and their owners.

Will returned shortly and said it was time. He gently lifted Codi from the blanket and carried him inside to a quiet room. Karen grabbed Codi's blanket and followed, eyes down, not wanting to look at the other dogs that were there. Other dogs that would be going home with their owners today to continue their normal lives. She followed Will into the office. Codi was placed on his blanket on the table. The vet spoke to them briefly, explaining with genuine compassion, how things would happen, and what to expect. He explained how Codi would receive two injections. One now, to relax and calm him, and a final one which would stop his heart. The vet administered the first needle and then left them alone with Codi for a few moments to say their final goodbyes. When he returned, second needle in hand, he asked if they were ready. Will nodded and the doctor looked to Karen. Tears began to fall as Karen nodded her ok. Then she knelt at Codi's head and looked straight into his eyes as the final needle was delivered. Karen watched as Codi's eyes began to droop, just as they always had when he dropped off to sleep. He opened them one last time after the final needle was given. Karen could feel his love and knew that he felt hers. She stroked his head and sobbed as his eyes closed once again for the last time. She continued to pet him while the vet used a stethoscope to check his heart. She laid her head against his, her tears wetting the soft brown fur, as the vet's words stabbed into her heart. "Codi's gone," he said quietly.

Since they had made previous arrangements to have his ashes returned to them for private burial, there was no further business to attend to. Dr. Jameson left them alone then, saying to take as much time as they needed, and to feel free to leave via the back door whenever they were ready. They remained with Codi for some time, hating so much to leave him there.   Eventually they gently removed his collar and gave him one last hug. It was over. "Thank you, Codi," Karen whispered. "Thank you for a job well done. We'll never forget you. Be happy, now. Goodbye dear friend."

For a good part of that day, Karen walked and walked in the rain, hardly aware that she was soaked right through. The cold and discomfort matched her mood. She knew that only time would ease the pain, but for now she accepted the heartache.

Chapter 4: Back at the shelter

After only a few days, Cujo found himself settling in quite nicely at the shelter. In fact, he rather enjoyed the freedom of his large kennel and his daily walks with gentle, caring people. Some of them worked at the shelter and some came in every now and then. The other dogs told him they were called volunteers, and that they came to visit the dogs here just to make them feel loved. Cujo had never known so many people who freely offered such kind words and frequent scratches behind the ears. He was so thankful not to be locked in that small space anymore. He still missed his people, however, especially his kids. But he had come to accept that they wouldn't be taking him home ever again. His heart felt a little sad by this, much as it had felt when he was taken from his mother and his sisters at the farm. It only hurt really bad for a while and then with time, you began to forget. You moved on and learned what was expected of you in your new life. Cujo wondered what his new life would be like after the shelter. Would he find new people in a forever home this time? Someone to love him as much as he wanted to love. Someone he could protect and stand by for all of his days? Cujo knew again, that only time would tell. What he didn't know, was how short a time he really had for that to happen.

Most dogs were only kept at the shelter for a few weeks. And for Cujo the clock had begun ticking down. Lots of people came to the shelter to look for new companions. Once a little girl and her dad took Cujo for a walk and stayed to pet him for quite a while. The little girl was just the kind of friend Cujo would love to have. He would walk by her side, sleep by her bed and take care of her in every way a dog could. He was so hopeful that they would take him home. But in the end, he heard those same human words that he had heard before. "He's just too big." He never saw the little girl again.

For several more long days, there were no visitors that stopped by Cujo's crate. He enjoyed hearing the other dogs bark with happiness as they left with happy new owners; for a dog knows no such thing as envy or jealousy, only joy for the good fortune of others. Maybe soon it would be his turn.

Chapter 5: Moving on

Karen couldn't believe that two weeks had passed since they had lost Codi.
She still felt him with her everywhere; in the car, at home, even when she
walked down the street. At times, she swore she could hear his nails click
clacking across the floor. She would turn, almost expecting to see him there.
She still expected to see him standing at the top of the stairs when she
finished her day, wagging his tail and waiting patiently for his walk. But she
also knew that the pain was growing softer. She could talk about him now
without crying, at least. She could laugh with family members about some of
the crazy things he had done. She knew she was healing. And she knew that
she was starting to miss having a dog around. Will had asked her several
times if she was ready to start thinking about another dog, but until now,
Karen had been emphatic in her refusal. Until now, it had seemed too soon.
It had seemed somehow disloyal to Codi. But Karen was beginning to sense
a change. Some little voice was telling her it was time to move on, that
maybe there was another dog out there that needed her and the love she had
to give. And then she had the dream. It was just her and Codi in the dream.
They were walking and playing as they always had, happy and smiling, but
there was one big difference. Codi was entirely white. In the dream, Karen
seemed oblivious to this fact. She knew only that Codi was running with her
like he had as a puppy, tail wagging and short little legs trying to keep up.
Karen awoke with such a feeling of contentment and peace. Although she
only told close family members about the dream, she believed it was an
omen. A sign from Codi that it was time to move on. Maybe today she
would suggest to Will that they just go see what dogs were at the shelter. "I
don't know for sure, that I'm ready," Karen said. "But let's just go see. I just
have a feeling that maybe we are meant to go today." When they arrived at
the shelter, they asked about the dogs that were available for adoption. As
the girl described several of the dogs, Karen listened but didn't feel like any
of them sounded quite right. Until she spoke of one particular rescue. "We
do have a dog who was surrendered about two weeks ago," she said as she
read from a clipboard of papers. He was left here February 10 by his
previous owners. Karen heard very little of her next words, struck by the fact
that this dog had been surrendered on the very day that they had had to put
Codi down. Karen felt sure that this was the connection she was waiting for.
This was the dog they were meant to have. "We would like to see that dog,"
Karen said. "He sounds perfect!"

Chapter 6: The Connection

The days moved on, and as much as he was comfortable at the shelter, Cujo began to feel very restless. He sensed that something new was coming his way. Then one day he felt an unusual sadness mixed with an odd kind of happiness in his belly. Something was different. He didn't understand what it was or where it was coming from but he knew that it meant there was a change coming for him. Somehow, somewhere the spirit of an unknown comrade was calling to him, telling him that soon, he would find his place and continue some very important work.

Sure enough, later that same day, a middle aged couple came to the shelter. They seemed to walk directly to his crate, bypassing several other dogs that wagged and wiggled and jumped and barked to get their attention. There was a sadness surrounding them, but it was tempered with a glimmer of hope and need. The woman person looked deep into his eyes and Cujo felt an immediate connection. This was the person he was meant to take care of. This was the person that his spirit companion was leading him to. Somehow he had to let her know that they were meant to be together. Since he was in the crate, he couldn't approach her and lean up against her to show his affection, so he did what he could. As she offered her hand through the bars of the crate, he licked it ever so gently, trying to show his love. Cujo watched as a different sensation appeared in the woman's eyes. It was love for sure and Cujo's heart almost burst. The couple left then, and Cujo was worried that they might not return. But the very next day the woman was back. She came alone this time to see him again. She stayed for only a short while but promised him that everything was going to be ok. He was going to be their dog and he was going to have the best life ever.

Sure enough, a few days later, the man person returned and Cujo was led out of his crate and into the care of the friendly, gentle man. He rode in the back seat of the car and he felt so wonderful. He was going to his forever home and he knew it. He could feel the spirit of the dog who had sat right here before him. He could feel all the positive love and energy that filled the air. As soon as he entered the house and met the woman person again, he knew he had absolutely nothing to fear. The spirit of the other dog was still here, waiting to pass the task of caring for his people over to Cujo. Cujo accepted the responsibility eagerly and made a promise to his departed companion that he would be loyal, loving and true to this family for all of his days on this earth. With that, the other spirit moved on and Cujo felt a happiness unlike anything he had ever felt before.

As the days went by, Cujo began to learn the routines and habits of the household. He was no longer called Cujo, but was renamed Riley. His people had smiled and made a joke about him having the "life of Riley." He didn't really know what that meant, but somehow he knew it was good.

And so it was. Riley lived out his life with the couple who had loved and cared for so many other dogs in their time. He continued the work that Codi and the others before him had begun. He was happy and content. He had found his forever home and it would be his until the time came to pass the job along to someone else. He hoped that day was a long way off.

The End

Turn the page to enjoy a free preview of Dana Lander's new work

"A Dog for Keeps"

A Dog for Keeps
©2012 Dana Landers
All Rights Reserved

Chapter 1

They said it would be the winter storm to top all winter storms. The snow had begun falling around noon and in just one hour it had started to build up thick on the roads. Julia knew the plows wouldn't be out until it was all over so it was definitely time to head home. She really wished that she had left work sooner, but it had taken a while to tie up the last loose ends of her latest offer. "I guess house closings have to happen snow or not," she thought to herself as she locked the office door. She knew the Emerson couple would be grateful that the final papers were signed, but that didn't change her prospect of a long, slow drive home. Fortunately, the office wasn't far from her house and the roads would be fairly well travelled by plenty of four wheel drive vehicles heading in the same direction. If you lived in Lilac Creek, you either had to have all wheel drive for the winter or plan to hibernate for five months.

Julia hit the unlock function on her fob and welcomed the shelter from the icy wind as she got in. Sitting for a few minutes to let things warm up gave her time to start thinking ahead to the chores that would be waiting at home. With a little luck she would make it down the driveway ok, but there would be some snow removal to be done sometime over the evening. Thankfully, this was usually a shared chore with her neighbor, Sam Baxter who lived in the other half of the old house she had fallen in love with and claimed as her own over three years ago.

It was one of the oldest homes in Lilac Creek, and one of the largest. Most of the homes were more like cottages, some of them stone, but many of them painted wood or cedar sided. The duplex Julia owned had once been an Inn where many a tourist had come to stay to enjoy a respite from the hustle and bustle of city life. When the old Inn closed, a couple had tried running it as a B&B for a while, but when they decided running a business was not their passion, they sold it to a local Doctor who lived in part of the house and converted the rest to offices and examining rooms. Old Dr. McKay ran his practice there for nearly thirty years before he retired to the sunny south and put it up for sale. Julia was asked to handle the listing when it came into the office, but the paperwork never went any further than her desk. She jumped on the chance to buy the old place and had plans for its conversion to a duplex settled in her mind before the ink had dried on the last piece of paper. Now she had her own cozy, country home and an income property as well. She thanked her lucky stars every day that she had also found a fantastic tenant for the other half of the house.

Her thoughts turned now to Sam Baxter and his daughter Brinn. The tragedy that they had suffered made Julia's heart ache every time she thought about it.

Suddenly a shrill sound broke her reverie and brought her back to matters at hand. The sounds of sirens on the highway just half a mile away chilled her even more than the gloomy storm. Someone had already fallen prey to the bad roads and Julia hoped it wasn't serious. "Better get going," she thought as she pulled slowly out of the parking lot. "It's going to get a lot worse before it gets better." Julia made her way out of town with no trouble and turned onto the first country road she would have to navigate. The snow banks were already a good two feet high from previous storms. "I'll be lucky if I can see over the banks at all when this one's finished," she muttered. The snow was heavy but there was no wind so she didn't have to worry about whiteout conditions. "Slow and steady," she kept repeating to herself. "Better to make it home in one piece than in good time!" On a good day the trip from town to the tiny hamlet of Lilac Creek took about 10 minutes. In bad weather like this, it could easily take a half hour or more. The roads were winding, hilly and narrowed by encroaching snow banks. Julia crept along and within about 20 minutes she was in sight of the turn onto her road. Tire tracks leading down the road told her that Sam was likely already home. He would have most likely picked Brinn up early from the daycare she attended in town. With any luck, that would mean his heavy duty Land Rover would have made track enough in the driveway for her to get in. She looked forward to a bit of down time with a steaming cup of coffee and some supper before heading out to help with snow removal.

To her surprise, the driveway was more than just a little cleared. There was only an inch or two of snow to drive through and the walkway to her door was cleared as well. Sam was just putting the snow blower into the garage as she drove up. Brinn was playing in the snow nearby, snow gear leaving nothing exposed but the smallest bit of her face. Her bright red and yellow toque was pulled down over her ears and a matching scarf covered her mouth. Julia waved to her as she pulled carefully into her side of the garage. Sam finished wiping down the snow blower and turned in her direction. "Glad to see you headed home a little early!" He said with some surprise. Sam knew what a workaholic she was. "Well, they said this was going to be a big one. Thought I'd get home ahead of the worst of it. Looks like you've been here for a while. Did they close the daycare early?"

Sam nodded. "I picked Brinn up a couple of hours ago. Thought I'd let her play outside for a bit while I got started on the snow."

Julia thanked him as she headed inside and promised to come out and help with the next round of clearing. "Hi sweetie," she said to Brinn as she passed by. The little girl said nothing. She glanced up from her play, and for just an instant her eyes met Julia's before turning downward once again.

Julia was still thinking about Brinn as she popped a dark roast K-Cup into her Keurig. She wished there was some way she could help. It saddened her to see a child so lost and broken, a child who should be laughing, playing and enjoying life. Instead she spent her days in silence, her voice stilled by the trauma that she no doubt relived over and over in her mind. Julia thought about how hard it had been for Sam to tell her the story. Her heart ached for him as well. She doubted there was a better father anywhere than her neighbor. She had certainly never witnessed dedication like his. His world revolved around Brinn and his only wish in life was to hear her sweet voice once again. Julia thought back to the day they met, when he had immediately explained the tragedy. "You should know," he had said. "If we're going to be neighbors, I want to be honest and open with you. I want you to understand why Brinn isn't like other kids" And so he had told her about the whole horrible tragedy.

Just over a year ago his wife Emily and her sister Gwen were driving home from a day of shopping. Brinn was in the back seat nestled among the day's wealth of store bought treasures. Emily had been born and raised here, in what a lot of people called "God's country." She loved the lakes, the rocks, the forests, and all the creatures that lived within their sanctuary. She was always mindful of them whenever she drove the country roads or the highway. In fact, she steadfastly refused to drive at dusk or after dark because those were the most dangerous times for animals and cars to collide. But this day it seemed, the fates had conspired against her. It was just late afternoon on a bright sunny August day when the one thing she had always feared, became her fate. She was driving carefully along the highway, watchful for wildlife that could run into the road at any moment. Unfortunately, one other driver was not so vigilant. Conditioned by years of predictable city driving, oblivious to the hazards of rural driving and travelling at a speed well above the limit, there was nothing he could do when a deer bounded out in front of his car. The high rate of speed at impact catapulted the large doe into the oncoming lane, hitting the windshield of Emily's car dead on. Emily and her sister were killed on impact. Brinn, secured in her car seat in the back was uninjured, but had to endure several traumatic minutes in the car with her Mom and Aunt before the paramedics arrived. When they arrived on the scene, Brinn was screaming hysterically for her Mommy. She was sedated and taken to hospital but released within hours. Yet, In spite of all the very best in medical treatment and counseling, she would not speak. Not even Sam's unshakable dedication and love could coax a sound from her tortured little soul.

Julia was thankful that Sam had shared the information with her. It had helped all of them form a strong and trusting friendship, one that made being good neighbors completely effortless. Julia took her cup from the hissing Keurig, added a few drops of cream and headed for the loveseat. Her plan was to enjoy her coffee and rest for a bit then bundle up to help shovel snow. Within minutes the coffee was gone and she had drifted off with her head back on the soft leather. A knock at the door startled her awake. She opened the door to a smiling Sam dressed in full outdoor attire. He had obviously finished up with the snow "I'm so sorry," she said. I must have drifted off.

"No worries," said Sam. "The snow stopped about a half hour ago. We're all good. Should be no trouble getting out in the morning."

"Great. Thanks, and again I'm sorry." Julia closed the door, thinking once again how lucky she was to have such a great neighbor.

Chapter 2

"Blasted winter!" grumbled the old man behind the wheel of his ancient pick-up. "One of these days I'm gonna move someplace where the snow don't fall for over half the year!" The black and tan mutt riding shotgun beside him barked in agreement. Henry Thompson lived alone in the house he had built many years ago when he and Alice were happy young newlyweds. Over the years they had added a screen porch to escape the torment of black flies and mosquitoes, expanded the kitchen to include and small breakfast set, and they had just recently finished an office area where Alice could work at her writing. It had started just as a hobby, but had grown into quite a passion. Henry teased her about getting lost in her books and forgetting all about him. It wasn't true, of course, but they loved to banter back and forth. It was always friendly, never hurtful and it was apparent to everyone who knew them that they remained sweethearts even after 50 years of marriage. Most of their days were passed with simple pleasure. A bit of fishing, model building and reading for Henry and gardening, reading, and most recently writing for Alice. They asked for little from those around them but gave much to anyone who needed their help or support. They had only one child, a daughter, Wendy, who now lived in California with her husband and their three beautiful grandkids. Alice had loved those kids with every ounce of her being. She called them often, sent parcels with special surprises for every special occasion, and recently had conquered her fear of the internet and had learned to use video calling. Even though thousands of miles separated them, they were very connected. Alice's new office was the hub of all that activity and it was what Alice called her happy place. But the office pretty much sat unused these days. Henry had no desire to even step inside its cozy confines. Alice had passed away from liver cancer six months ago and her writings remained unfinished. The computer sat unopened, and little items that had been collected for mailing sat waiting. He supposed he would have to tend to all of those things someday, but that day just hadn't come yet. The day had not yet come when he would consider selling the house and maybe moving out to the coast to be near Wendy and the kids. She was always urging him to at least come for a visit, and he hadn't done that yet either. When Wendy had come home for her mother's funeral they had talked at length about what his future might hold. But he wasn't ready to do anything just yet. Most of the time, he felt like Alice was still there with him, as if he was just waiting for her to get home from some shopping trip or cooking class. He felt her presence so strongly still, that the thought of leaving felt too much like leaving her behind. He knew that time would change all that, and he was willing to let that time pass at its own speed.

For now, he had more urgent matters to deal with; this winter storm being the main one. Henry didn't usually venture out on the roads in any kind of bad weather, but he had run out of some things and wanted to get stocked up in case the storm turned out to be as big as they expected. You just couldn't trust the weather reporters to get it right. Sometimes they predicted a whopper and they ended up having flurries. And sometimes the flurries they said to expect turned into blizzards. At any rate, Henry preferred to rely on his old achy bones to tell him what was coming, and today his joints were telling him this was going to be a big one! He was pretty good at keeping his cupboards stocked during the winter, but he had been laid up for a while with a cough and fever. Now his supplies were low and another storm was hitting hard. He hunched right over top of the steering wheel and kept his eyes glued right to the road. "Keep an eye out there, Jasper, old boy," he said to the dog. "Don't want to be going off into the ditch now do we?" As if he

understood exactly what the old man was saying, Jasper kept his
eyes focused on some point in the distance ahead of the car.
Though there was no wind to add to the poor visibility, the snow
was coming down hard, creating that hypnotic effect that can be
dangerous and distracting. Henry drove slowly, using the white
line on his right to judge where the road was going. He was a bit
disoriented and thought that they should be getting close to his
driveway by now. He couldn't remember crossing the wooden
bridge over Lilac Creek, or the big curve that came right
afterwards. Thinking that he was maybe going a lot slower than
was necessary, he decided to pick up the pace a bit, He put just a
little more pressure on the gas and his old Chevy lurched forward.
His thoughts were now on getting home. Suddenly out of the white
whirling storm, the curve in the road that he had thought he already
passed appeared, but Henry was moving too fast to take it. The
truck began to fishtail. Panicking, Henry hit the brake and the
truck began to slide. Instead of rounding the curve it went straight
ahead, off the road and into a tree. The impact crumpled the front
end and pushed the doors wide open. Jasper had been thrown to the
floor when Henry hit the brakes and after a few seconds of
confusion, climbed into the small crunched space that had been the
front seat. His master was slumped over the twisted steering
wheel. He nosed Henry's arm and whimpered. When he got no
response, he started licking Henry's face. When that failed to rouse
his master, he spread himself across Henry's lap. After a time,
Jasper started feeling cold and thirsty. He knew there was
something seriously wrong with Henry, and he knew what he had
to do. Feeling a little stiff from the cramped space and his fall to
the floor, Jasper crawled slowly down from the truck. He didn't
know where he was but he had a sense that home was not far off.
If he could find the way to his road, there were friends there who
would help Henry. And so, sore and snow covered, he started out

into the storm.

~

Buy this book now at Amazon.com

ISBN 9798530122446

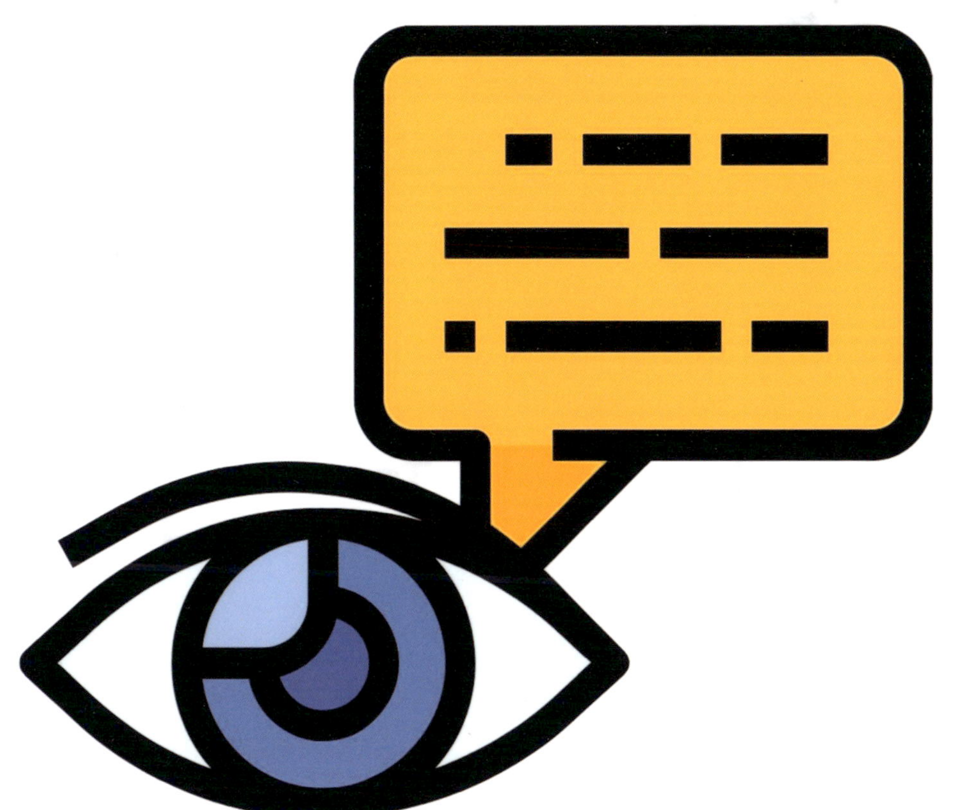

PROLONGED EYE CONTACT

What It Means And How's It Important